Changing Weather

Written by George Ivanoff

macmillan
ecucation

Look at the sky.
What is the weather
like today?

Sometimes it is hot.

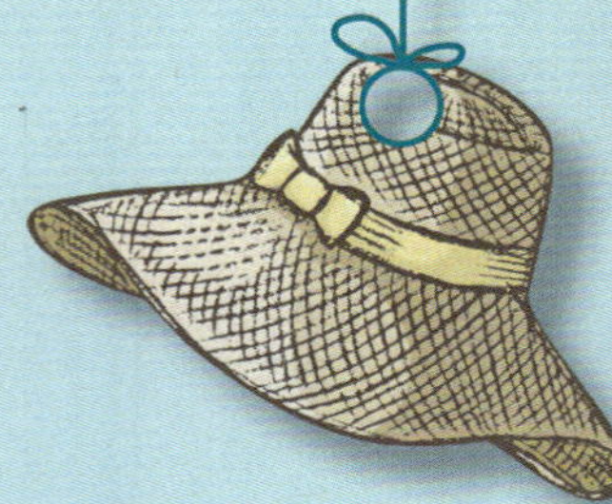

A t-shirt and hat can keep you cool.

Sometimes it is cold.

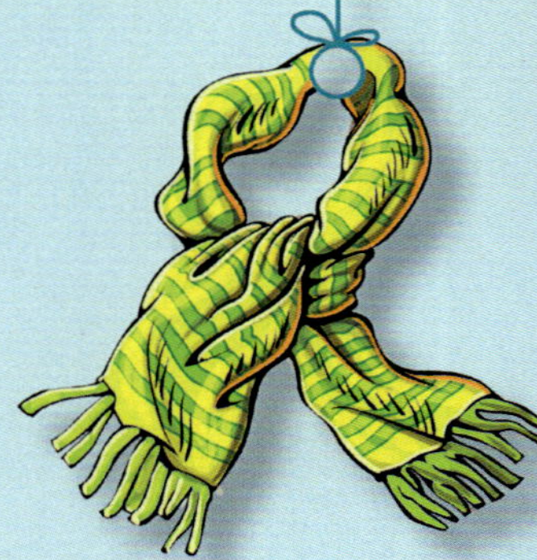

A coat and scarf can
keep you warm.

Sometimes it is rainy.

A raincoat and boots can keep you dry.

What to Wear	
Weather	**Clothes**
hot	 
cold	 
rainy	 

After Reading

Let's Think About It

- What did you already know about the weather? What did you learn from reading the text?
- Why is it important to dress properly for different types of weather?
- What is your favourite type of weather? Why?

Let's Talk About It

Share your answers with your group.

- I already knew that ... I learnt ...
- It is important to dress properly for the weather because ...
- My favourite type of weather is ... because ...

Which was your favourite answer?